FABULOUS Fashions

Coloring Book

COLOR TEST PAGE

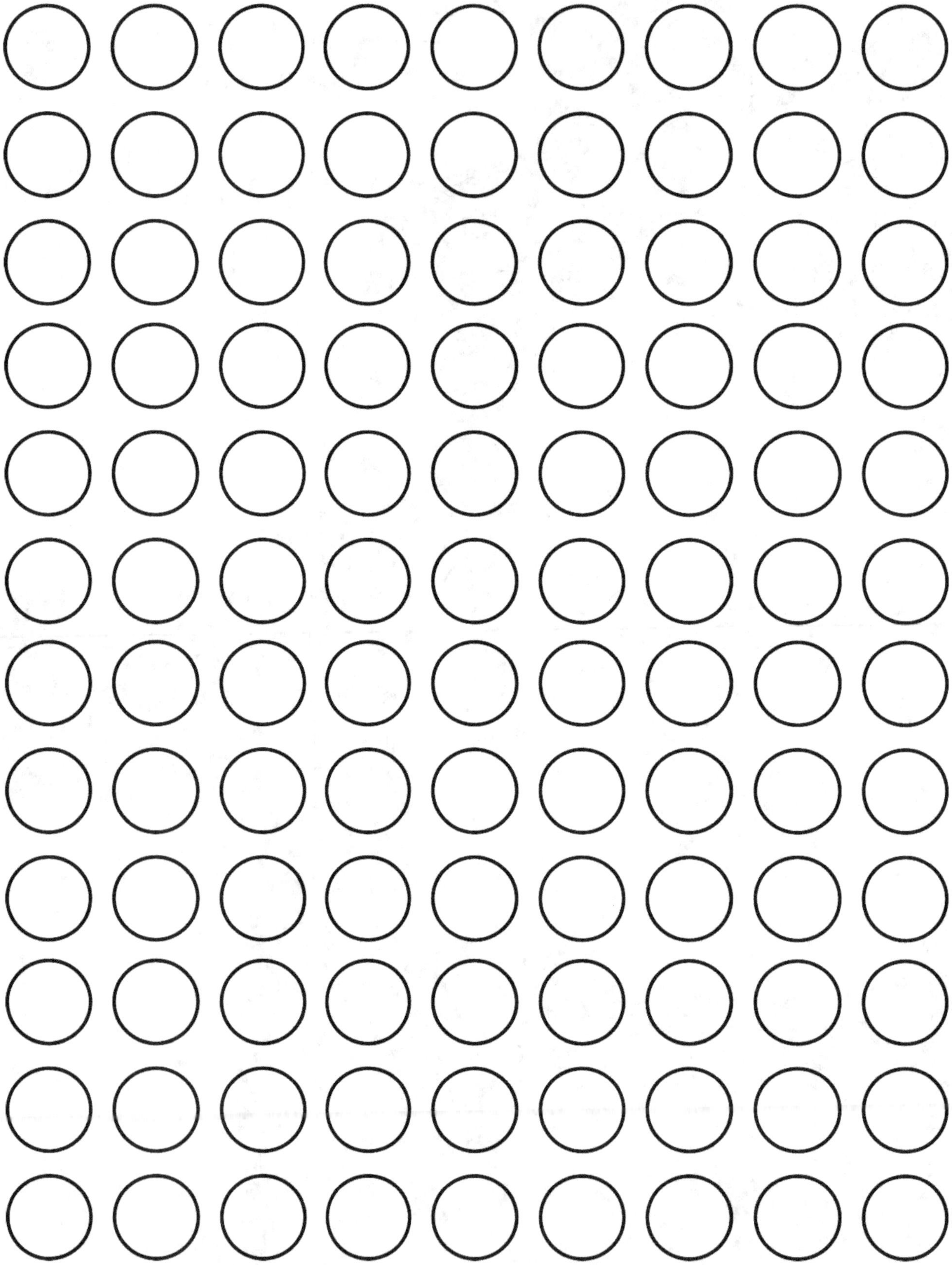

COLOR TEST PAGE

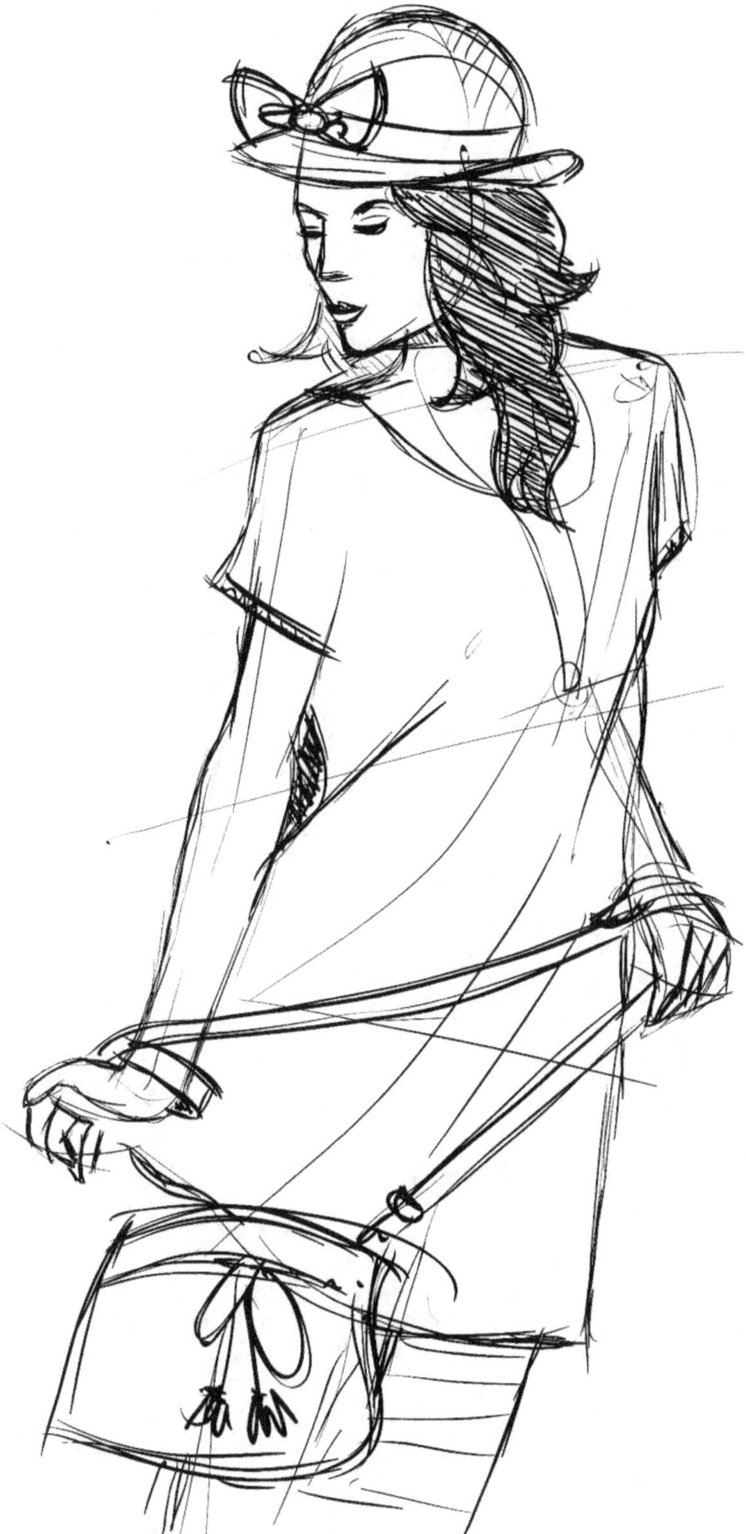

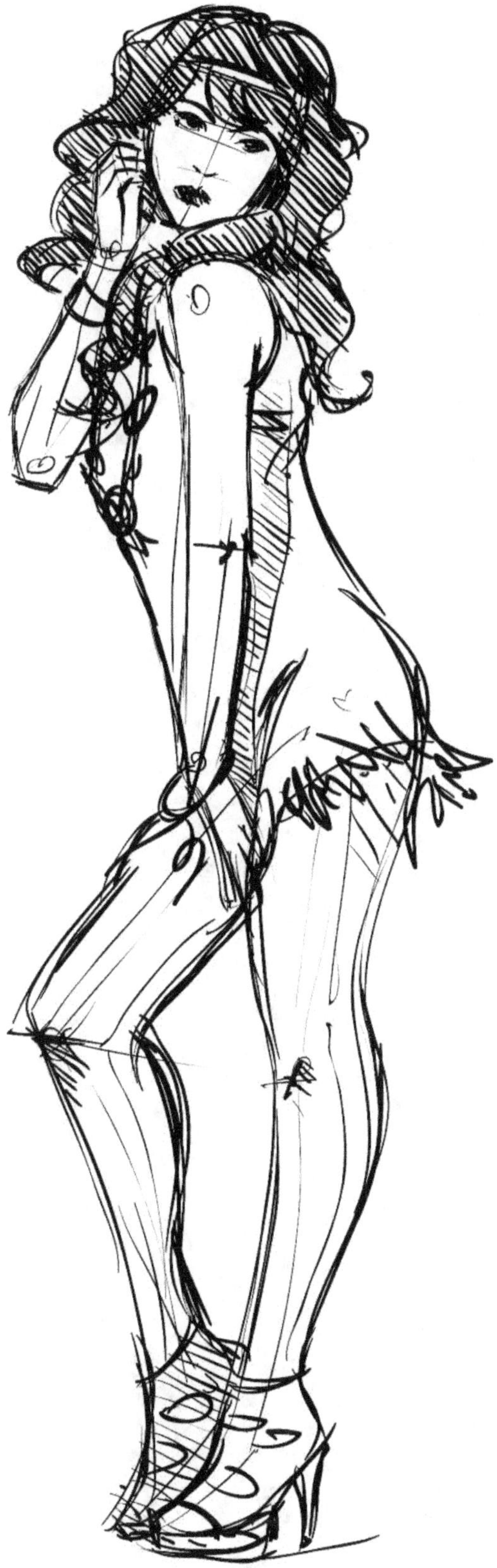

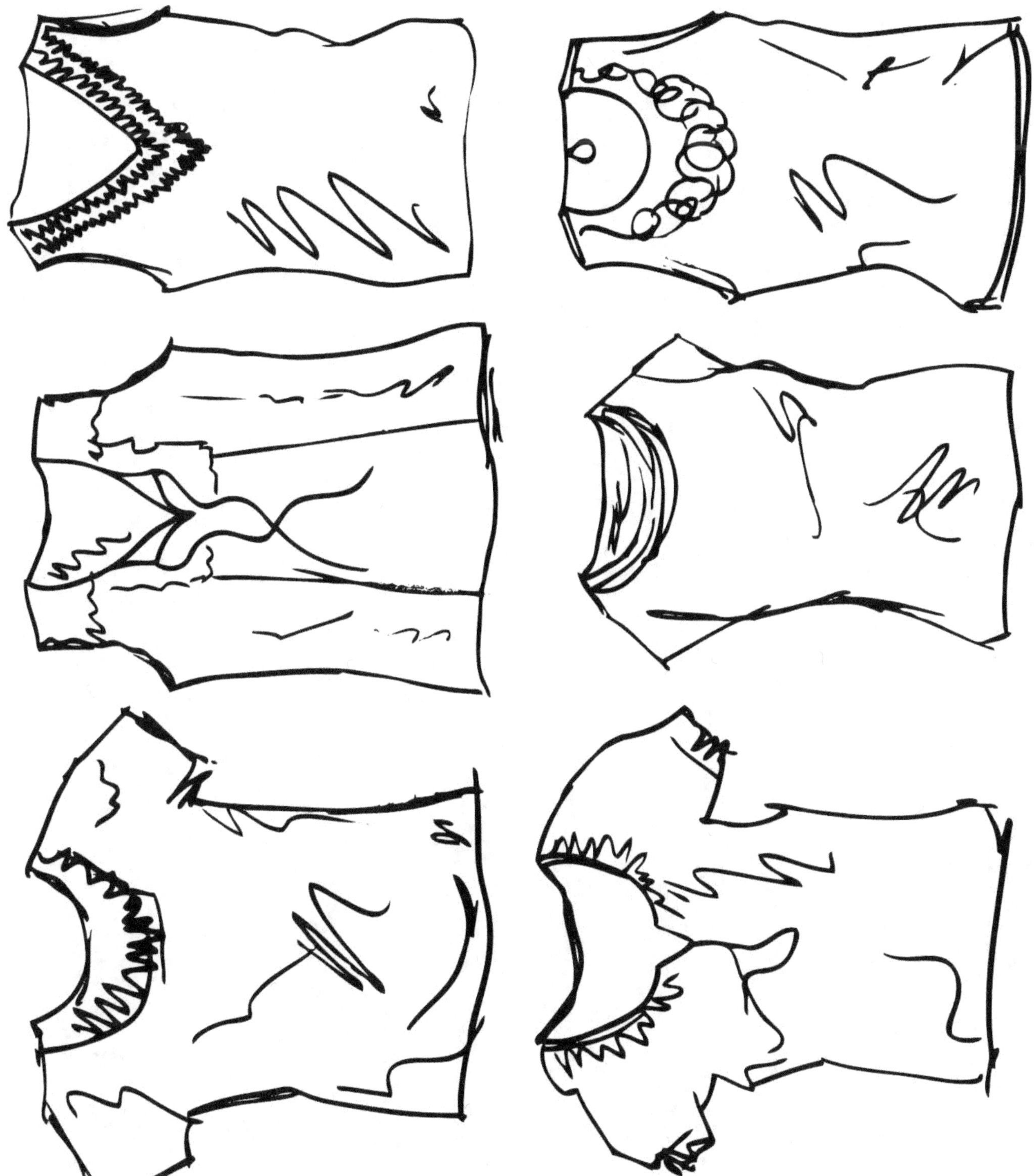

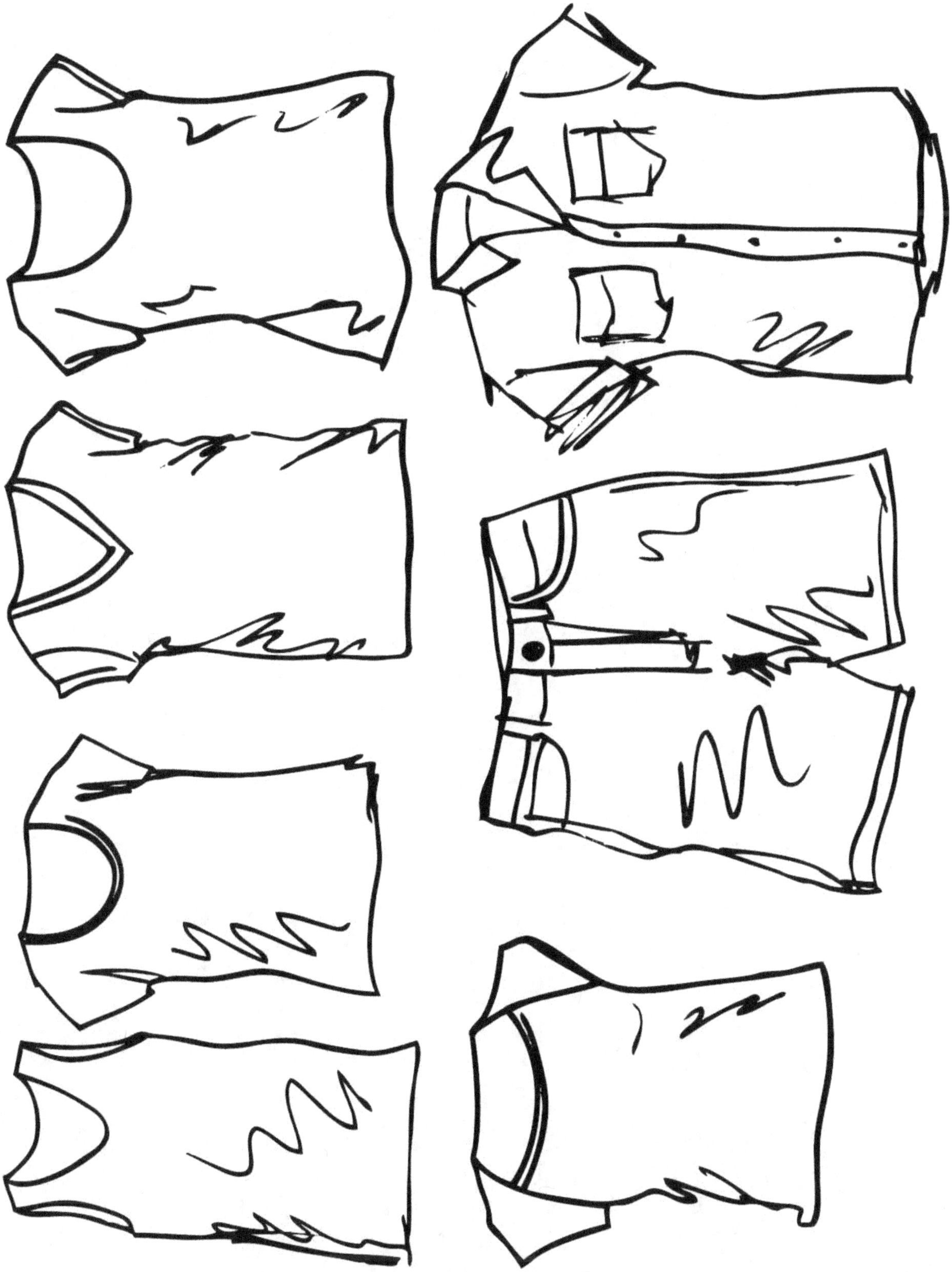

www.ingramcontent.com/pod-product-compliance
Lightning Source LLC
Chambersburg PA
CBHW081245280526
45787CB00006B/2804

* 9 7 8 1 5 3 5 1 6 5 0 1 3 *